Blue Willow

Mary Frank Gaston

COLLECTOR BOOKS
A Division of Schroeder Publishing Co., Inc.

The current values in this book should be used only as a guide. They are not intended to set prices, which vary from one section of the country to another. Auction prices as well as dealer prices vary greatly and are affected by condition as well as demand. Neither the Author nor the Publisher assumes responsibility for any losses that might ber incurred as a result of consulting this guide.

Additional copies of this book may be ordered from:

COLLECTOR BOOKS
P.O. Box 3009
Paducah, Kentucky 42001

or

The Author: Mary Frank Gaston
P.O. Box 342
Bryan, Texas 77806

@$9.95. Add $1.00 for postage and handling.

Copyright: Mary Frank Gaston, 1983
ISBN: 0-89145-231-1

DEDICATION

To Jerry and Jeremy

ACKNOWLEDGEMENTS

As with most books, the final product is rarely accomplished without assistance from others. This one is no exception, and I sincerely appreciate the contributions, assistance, and encouragement of the following individuals. First my family: my husband, Jerry, did all of the photography for the book in addition to taking me across the country to obtain information. He also edited the manuscript. Our 11 year old son, Jeremy Gaston, helped with the proofing of the manuscript, and also had to forego many of the activities he would have preferred doing when he had to accompany us on photographing trips! My mother, Vera Ballow, helped in many ways at home.

Lois Misiewicz, Fallbrook, California, generously helped from the very first, not only by allowing me to photograph her extensive collection, but by suggesting names of collectors, and providing invaluable information and insights through *The Willow Notebook* which she publishes. Connie Rogers, Dayton, Ohio, deserves my gratitude for her contributions in *The Willow Notebook*, *National Journal*, and *Depression Glass Daze* on Blue Willow as well as letting me personally "pick her brain" about marks and patterns. She also provided a lovely collection to photograph. I thank Conrad Biernacki, Toronto, Canada, for his articles in *The Willow Notebook* and the *National Journal* relating to Blue Willow, and for corresponding with me to help with this project. I am especially indebted to Conrad and Connie's work on Willow pattern identification which I use here, and which makes, I think, a very important contribution to the study of Blue Willow. John Macy, Houston, Texas, so kindly shared his truly varied collection with us. His pieces really gave me the idea for my "Alphabet" approach for this Blue Willow book. The items featured on the cover are also courtesy of John Macy.

Special thanks go to Glenwood and Martha Vernon, Brenham, Texas, for providing their large collection of Booth's pattern for photographs. I also thank Gladys M. Donham, Houston, Texas; Dunn & Ross Antiques, Houston, Texas; Grandfather's Trunk, Deland, Florida; Jesse and Harry Hall, Springboro, Ohio; Charlene and Don Johnson, Golden Age Antiques, Pawnee, Oklahoma; Nickerson's Antiques, Eldon, Missouri; Martha Schow, Trading Fair II, Houston, Texas; Carl Schluter and John Savell, S and S Outpost, Wallis, Texas; and Bettye Whitmire, Pastyme Antiques, Irving, Texas for permitting me to photograph their Blue Willow.

PREFACE

Although the Blue Willow pattern on ceramics has been criticized since its invention, criticism has not deterred the loyal devotees of this most popular of all patterns. The design has managed to hold its own quite well for nearly two hundred years. The popularity of the pattern has not faded with time or life style changes as fads and fashions usually do. Today, companies in many countries including America, England, and Japan manufacture all types of ceramic articles decorated with the Blue [or often some other color] Willow pattern. Additionally, one can find a myriad of other contemporary objects ranging from plastics to linens with this distinctive blue and white design.

People have collected Blue Willow throughout its history, but the pattern's collectability is probably at its height today. The number of collectors is constantly increasing--and in an organized manner too. "Willow" clubs for "Willowers" are found in towns throughout the United States and also in Canada. A bi-monthly newsletter, *The Willow Notebook* is published by Lois K. Misiewicz. The newsletter keeps collectors abreast of rarities, prices, marks, and new products as well as specialized items for collectors such as stationery and even blue and white stained glass turtle doves! The newsletter also acts as an outlet for collectors to buy and sell Blue Willow through classified advertising. [For information concerning Willow Clubs and *The Willow Notebook*, please send a SASE to Lois K. Misiewicz, 6543 Indian Trail, Fallbrook, California 92028.]

This book is designed to show a wide range of antique and collectable Blue Willow. An adequate supply of such items is still available for collectors. Because of the number and diversity of articles exhibiting this pattern, the photographs are laid out in ABC fashion by type of item. Some contemporary items and a few non-ceramic items are included to demonstrate the unending passion for the Blue Willow pattern. Today's items will surely find their niche in antique history during the next two hundred years!

A section on manufacturer's marks precedes the color photographs of objects. A glossary of terms pertinent to ceramics that might prove beneficial to collectors is included at the end of the book. A price range is quoted for items illustrated in the book. Please keep in mind that prices are influenced by a multitude of factors including condition, availability, and demand. Ultimately the collector must be the judge of the value of a particular piece. The prices shown in this book are intended to be used only as a guide. Price information was obtained from dealers, collectors, sales, and shops throughout the United States in order to give as accurate a reflection as possible of current Blue Willow prices. Figures stated assume that items are in good-to-mint condition.

I hope you enjoy browsing through the Blue Willow Alphabet. If you have or find a "Z" Blue Willow collectable, please let me know! (But please include a SASE when writing.)

Mary Frank Gaston
P. O. Box 342
Bryan, Texas 77806

4

CONTENTS

THE BLUE WILLOW LEGEND

The story on the back of this book is but one of many legends connected with the ceramic items displaying the popular Blue Willow pattern. The stories vary in length and content--some are short, some are long, some are simple, and some are quite elaborate. Because there are so many, I cannot reproduce them all here.

The elements that make up the overall design of the Willow pattern, however, all have a special significance in each legend, but the essence of each is usually quite similar: A wealthy Chinese father (usually referred to as the Mandarin) wishes his daughter (Hong Shee, Koong-shee, or Li-chi are some of the names for her) to marry a man he has chosen (his accountant or secretary, or a duke or an older person of wealth and prestige). The daughter, however, is in love with a young man (usually called Chang). The young lovers decide to run away before the prearranged marriage takes place. They are not completely successful, for depending on the particular legend, the couple is eventually pursued either by the father or the bridegroom-to-be, or Chang is killed by the bridegroom, or both Chang and the daughter die. The couple is not destined to be parted, though, for ultimately in most legends the gods change the two into a pair of turtle doves so that they may be together forever.

People enjoy collecting these various stories as well as the dishes with the Blue Willow pattern they describe. When comparing the story to the design on a plate, the pattern does seem to come to life. You find yourself actually believing the legend through its illustration.

But turning from legend to fact, it is interesting to note that the Blue Willow legends were not created until after the Blue Willow pattern on china became popular. Also the legends are not Chinese in origin as is sometimes thought. The stories were invented by the English and Americans. And the pattern, as we know it, was designed by the English and not the Chinese.

HISTORY OF THE BLUE WILLOW PATTERN

Although the Blue Willow pattern was not originally designed by the Chinese, its inspiration, of course, definitely was influenced by the Chinese. The major components of the pattern, namely the willow tree, the orange tree, and tea house all relate to Oriental culture. These elements had been used by the Chinese for centuries to decorate their porcelain wares. The English as well as other West Europeans greatly admired the beautiful porcelain which had been imported from China since the 1600's. Those items were decorated with hand-painted blue underglaze Oriental themes. Attempts were made again and again in Europe to reproduce those items, both in body and decoration. Efforts were not successful, though, until the mid 1700's.

The successful evolution of the Blue Willow pattern was due to two factors: one, the transfer method of decoration, and two, the technique of underglaze decoration. (Please see the Glossary for a description of these terms.) Although pottery as an industry was started in the Staffordshire district of England in the mid 1600's, the products were earthenware and not translucent porcelain like the Chinese wares. The English ceramics of this period were decorated by hand and over the glaze. Transfer printed designs and underglaze decoration were not in use in England until after 1760.

6

The transfer method of decoration allowed the same design or pattern to be used over and over again. It could be applied either over or under the glaze and used on any type of ceramic body. This method of decoration was much less expensive than hand painting. Decoration could be more elaborate, and many and all kinds of objects could be decorated with the same pattern. The technique of transfer designs over the glaze was practiced in England during the 1750's.

It was not until the 1760's, however, that the method of transfer printing under the glaze was perfected. Underglaze printing was preferred to overglaze printing because it made the pattern permanent. Decoration over the glaze could be marred or worn off. The Chinese had known the technique of underglaze decoration for hundreds of years, and the products imported from China had handpainted underglaze decoration. The Chinese had discovered that the color blue, derived from cobalt, was the one color which could withstand the high degrees of heat necessary to fire the glaze and still maintain the clarity of the design. That is why the oriental porcelains were decorated with blue and white designs. That is also why the Blue Willow pattern originated in blue rather than in some other color. So, the English, wanting to copy the Chinese style, designs, and colors, discovered it was necessary to use the color blue if they wanted underglaze decoration.

Thomas Turner of the Caughley Pottery in Staffordshire is usually credited with being the first (circa 1780) to engrave a Willow pattern, and transfer it underglaze. Thomas Minton, an apprenticed engraver for the Caughley factory and later a master engraver in London, also designed Willow patterns at about that time. But the Spode factory, not Turner or Minton, is attributed as the inventor (circa 1790) of the pattern that ultimately became the traditional Blue Willow pattern.

According to Robert Copeland, in his book *Spode's Willow Pattern and other Designs after the Chinese*, the traditional Blue Willow pattern is actually Spode's Willow III which was designed circa 1810. Spode's original Willow I and II (designed around 1790) differ from the Traditional pattern (Willow III) chiefly in the border designs and method of engraving the transfer pattern.

Copeland also notes, as do others, that the term "Willow" was used for ceramics decorated with Oriental themes prior to the Spode designs. But there is no consensus about when the term originated or why the earliest English Oriental patterns and later Spode's patterns were called "Willow" in the first place. The patterns could have been called by other names of other designs featured in the pattern.

My guess is that the term "Willow" evolved as a pattern name because the tree form used by the Chinese for decoration on their porcelain was the most recognizable to the English of any of the decoration themes on Oriental wares. Thus, they called the tree form "Willow", eventually using the term to describe patterns containing such a tree form design.

Once the methods of transfer printing and underglaze decoration were perfected, the English potters were in a good position to compete with the Oriental imported ceramic goods. They could manufacture all of the blue and white dishes that the English desired, and most importantly at a price they could afford. An enormous market was available for the products, not only in England but in America and Canada as well.

During the 1800's most English potteries produced a version of the Blue Willow pattern. The pattern was applied to all classes of ceramics beginning with semi-porcelain in the early days and later extending to stoneware, ironstone, and bone china. These terms concerning the body types of ceramics are defined in the Glossary. Knowledge of the different body types is important for collectors. The body type may determine the condition of a particular piece and in turn its desirability and its price. By becoming familiar with the characteristics of the various classes of ceramics, one is often able to distinguish the old from the new, and to determine the country of origin if the example is not marked.

England was the first country to manufacture Blue Willow. However, many other countries also followed suit. Japan is probably the next largest producer of the pattern. Many examples from that country were imported to the United States from the late 1880's to the present. Potteries in the United States also manufactured a large amount of the pattern during the 20th century, especially during the 1920's and 1930's. Examples are also seen from Belgium, France, Germany, Holland, Ireland, Mexico, Poland, Portugal, and Spain. And, although the Chinese did not design the Blue Willow pattern originally, Oriental potters did use the pattern for decorating ceramics after it became so popular in England!

BLUE WILLOW PATTERNS

The traditional Blue Willow pattern is considered to be the one designed by Spode. However, when people say they collect Blue Willow, that does not usually mean that they collect only pieces with the Traditional (Spode type) pattern. Numerous other versions of the Willow pattern have been manufactured through the years by other companies in England as well as companies in other countries. There are probably about as many, if not more, versions of the Blue Willow pattern as there are versions of the legend connected with the pattern. There is not just *one* Blue Willow legend, likewise there is not just *one* Blue Willow pattern.

Some years ago, I personally learned that all Blue Willow patterns are not the same. I had just opened an antique business specializing in all types of dinner services. One day a lady brought in a Blue Willow plate. She needed one more to complete a dinner service for eight. I told her I would try to find such a plate for her, and carefully made a note of the manufacturer's mark. While on a buying trip, I did indeed find a Blue Willow plate. Returning home, I immediately called the lady who promptly came (from some distance, too) to pick up her plate. However, my plate did not *exactly* match hers even though it had the same mark. Needless to say, she was very disappointed. I learned that in the future I must really look closely at the details of the Blue Willow pattern I was trying to match and not just the maker's mark--for often the same maker made more than one version of that pattern!

The traditional Blue Willow pattern contains many components. (See Plate 195 for one example). The outer border is composed of several scroll and geometric designs. An inner border of geometric designs frames the center pattern. This center pattern features a tea house with a pavillion on the right side. An orange tree (often called an apple tree) is behind the tea house. A willow tree is almost centered in the design. In front of the willow tree is a bridge with three people. A boat with a person in it is to the top left of the willow tree, and above the boat is another Oriental style building and a fir tree. A zig-zag fence is at the bottom of the design, and two birds facing each other are at the top of the pattern.

Many manufacturers used transfers with the exact version of this Spode pattern or altered it only slightly. But other companies had their own interpretation of the pattern. Also, as I noted, some potteries manufactured more than one version of the pattern. We find that some Blue Willow patterns have no birds while others have flocks. Also the shape, size, and direction of flight of the birds may vary. The number of the people in the pattern many range from none to four. The shape of the bridge may differ as well as the position of the buildings, willow tree, and boat, and there may be more than one boat in the pattern. Some patterns are reversed by having usual right-handed components of the pattern on the left and vice versa. Sometimes only a part of the willow design is used to decorate items. The blue color may range from very dark to quite light, or the pattern may not be blue at all, but some other color or group of colors.

Because of such variations, it appears at first glance that it would be impossible to find any points of similarity for the different willow patterns manufactured by so many different companies throughout the years. But that is not really so. Many of the willow pattern variations do have some basic features in common that are related to border and center design.

Conrad Biernacki and Connie Rogers, both advanced Willow collectors, have done extensive work in categorizing these different borders and center patterns. Although they note that the categories are not all-inclusive for every willow pattern ever made, I find that the categories are quite helpful not only for collectors who are trying to match pieces, but also for beginning collectors to acquaint them with the different willow patterns. I also think that being able to categorize many of the willow patterns adds another interesting dimension to this field of collecting.

I use these categories to describe chiefly (with a few exceptions) the plates and platters illustrated in the photographs of this book. The variations and pattern components are easier to see and understand on items with flat surfaces than they are on rounded bodies such as bowls, cups, and pitchers, especially when looking at a photograph. Thus the following terms and numbers for categories of Willow Pattern Borders and Center Patterns are those used in articles by Conrad Biernacki in the *National Journal* and by Conrad Biernacki and Connie Rogers in the *Willow Notebook* which are listed here in the Bibliography. I have included brief descriptions of these categories and indicated one photograph example of each, but please see these articles and Robert Copeland's *Spode's Willow Pattern and other Designs after the Chinese* for more detailed descriptions and historical information.

WILLOW BORDER PATTERNS

1. **TRADITIONAL.** This border is the Spode border design for Willow II. A wheel or circular design is the main characteristic of this pattern. See Plate 195.
2. **BUTTERFLY** or **INSECT** or **FITZHUGH.** This border is named for the winged antennaed designs in the pattern, or called "Fitzhugh" for a person by that name who supposedly commissioned a set of china to be made with this particular style of border. See Plate 159.
3. **BOW KNOT.** Four-section loop shapes characterize this border. See Plate 137.
4. **DAGGER** or **FLEUR-DE-LIS.** Tiny Pointed designs are on the inside of the border pointed toward the center pattern. See Plate 149.

5. **SCROLL** and **FLOWER**. Fancy curved designs are combined with floral patterns. See Plate 163.

6. **FLORAL**. This type of border is composed chiefly of floral designs. See Plate 143.

7. **PICTORIAL**. Miniature or cameo willow pattern designs compose the outer border. See Plate 166.

8. **SIMPLE LINE**. Only one or two solid colored ring type or a series of short lines form the border. See Plates 43 and 207.

9. **BORDERLESS**. These patterns have no outer border. See Plate 196.

Mr. Biernacki notes that there are variations in the border patterns, especially in the Scroll and Flower, Floral, and Pictorial categories. He suggests that one should also indicate the name of the manufacturer, if known, and any pattern name that might be included in the mark when describing items with these types of borders that differ from the one most commonly seen.

WILLOW CENTER PATTERNS

1. **TRADITIONAL**. This is the center pattern referred to earlier that is based on the original Spode design for their Willow III. This is the most common willow center pattern. The pattern is characterized by 4 figures, 2 birds, 1 boat, and the willow and orange tree. There is also an innner border of geometric designs. Mr. Biernacki notes that the Japanese versions of the Traditional pattern do not usually have this inner border. See Plate 195.

2. **BOOTHS**. This center pattern is named for the pattern used by the Booth Company in England. It has a Butterfly Border. TWO PHOENIX or DOUBLE PHOENIX are the names denoting the Japanese copies of this particular pattern. See Plates 137 and 189 for a comparison.

3a. **TWO TEMPLES I**. This center pattern is based on and named for an original Spode design also. Two seemingly overlapping temples on the left of the pattern, 4 figures (two on the bridge, one in temple doorway, one on rocks) and no birds characterize this rendition of the willow pattern. It has a Butterfly border. See Plate 151.

3b. **TWO TEMPLES II**. This center pattern is also one of Spode's originals as #3a. It is similar to Two Temples I except there are only 3 figures (two on the bridge, one in temple doorway) in the design, and the Butterfly border is not exactly the same. This version of Two Temples is more common than Two Temples I. Sometimes the pattern is reversed. See Plate 159.

4. **MANDARIN II**. This is another center pattern based on an original Spode design. This pattern has 3 figures but no orange tree. It has a Dagger border. See Plate 149.

5. **WORCESTER**. This center pattern is named for the pattern used by the Worcester Royal Porcelain Company, England. It has 3 figures and 3 boats but no orange or willow tree. It has a Scroll and Flower border. See Plate 178.

6. **BURLEIGH**. This pattern is named for one design found on items manufactured by the English company of Burgess and Leigh. The pattern has 3 figures but no orange tree. It has a Scroll and Flower border. See Plate 220.

7. **TURNER**. This pattern is named for the Turner Company in England. It has 2 figures in the design and no birds. It has a Scroll and Flower border. See Plate 163.

8. **SIMPLIFIED.** This category is for versions of the willow pattern that show only a part of the pattern. They may have a Floral, Pictorial, or Simple Line border, or no border at all. See Plate 213.

9. **POLYCHROME.** This term denotes any multi-colored variant pattern. See Plate 171.

10. **CANTON.** This category of pattern includes the early handpainted Chinese patterns and also the English copies of these patterns. See Plate 142 for an example of the Chinese pattern and Plates 162 and 177 for English copies of the pattern.

In using these Border and Center Pattern categories to describe the photographs of plates, I use the Traditional term if the essential elements for that pattern are basically the same: the number and position of buildings, willow and orange tree, bridge, people, birds, and boat. As I noted, some of the renditions of the Traditional category appear to have some variations as to shape of trees, boat, people, birds, etc. They are not considered variants, however, unless, for example, the pattern has four birds rather than two.

I use the term "Two Temples Variant" to describe examples of this pattern that may be Simplified but also have only two figures, or have birds which are not the characteristics of either Two Temples I or II. However, they still have "two temples" as the dominating characteristic. Likewise, I refer to the Simplified pattern of Two Temples II as Two Temples II Simplified rather than just Simplified to further identify the pattern. In most instances I do not use category 9 (Polychrome) alone if one of the center patterns is identifiable as one of the Center categories or a variant of one. I include that information also in the description.

DATING BLUE WILLOW

A particular version of the Blue Willow pattern usually cannot be used as a guide for dating specific pieces. There has really been no time period, even in the early years, when just one Blue Willow pattern was manufactured. Also the various components that make up the pattern such as the number of oranges (or apples) on the tree, the shape of the bridge or buildings, the number of people, or presence or absence of birds, or the fence in the design cannot be used for dating the pattern. Copeland notes that the blue of the early patterns was quite dark, but through the years manufacturing processes became more sophisticated which allowed the pattern to be produced in all shades of blue. This holds true for today as well with the pattern being seen in various blue shades.

Many pieces of Blue Willow were not marked by the manufacturer, especially during the early period. Marks, however, are perhaps the most accurate method of finding out the time period for many of the examples available to the collector. If the piece is unmarked, the body of the object often gives a clue to the period of manufacture. Familiarity with the various body types and glazes can be accomplished by examining marked examples of the pattern from the early, middle, and late periods. Knowledge gained from such examination will provide good clues to help in determining whether an unmarked piece was made ten, fifty, or a hundred years ago.

Manufacturers' marks usually do not tell you the exact year a specific piece was made, but the time period a mark was in use can often be known. Most collectors like to know as much as possible about what they collect. Knowledge of the time a particular company used a certain mark and the beginning and closing dates of a company aid in this search.

The mark of the manufacturer is found on the back or base of an object in one of three forms: incised, impressed or printed. (See the Glossary for a description of these terms). Incised, impressed, and underglaze printed marks are basically considered to be permanent, meaning that they cannot be worn off or taken off. Sometimes examples are seen where this has been attempted, either by grinding out the mark, or placing another mark over the original one. This is especially true for items of Japanese or German origin following World War II. English marks are found in all three forms appearing either singly or in combination. The majority are printed, however. American, Japanese, and most other countries' marks on Blue Willow are of the printed type.

Because of extensive and intensive research, namely by England's Geoffrey A. Godden, Blue Willow of English origin is perhaps easier to date than examples from other countries. Because such a large portion of Blue Willow was made in England, collectors should be aware of several points which can help in interpreting English marks.

A rope-like symbol shaped like a bow is sometimes seen printed on English ceramics. The mark may or may not contain initials which can identify the company of manufacture. This symbol is known as the Staffordshire Knot because it was used by many potteries in the Staffordshire district of England.

An impressed or printed diamond symbol with letters and numbers or just printed numbers prefaced with the initials "RD" are sometimes found on items either alone or combined with other types of marks. Such marks indicate that the pattern or mold (shape) of the object was registered with the English Patent Office in order to keep that particular pattern or mold from being copied by some other manufacturer. The diamond mark was instituted in 1843, and when decoded, the month, day, and year of registration can be determined. This system continued until 1883. In 1884, a consecutive numbering system starting with "RD1" replaced the former method. General books on marks usually give the tables for decoding the diamond symbol, and also show what numbers the patents had reached on the first of January of each year starting with 1885 through about 1900 for the consecutive numbering system. Thus, if an example has and "RD" number that falls between the numbers listed for January of 1885 and January 1886, the design was registered sometime during 1885.

These English registry marks are often misinterpreted. The dates refer to the time the design or shape was *first* registered--not when a particular piece was *made*. The piece had to be made after the design was registered so that the manufacturer would know what letters or numbers to put on the piece. But it is often stated that from the diamond shape one can date *exactly* pieces so marked, or from the registry number, the exact year the piece was made can be known. The first pieces of a particular registered design or shape may have been made during the year shown by the mark, but not on that day of the month decoded from the diamond shape registry mark. Most importantly, the same design or shape may have been used for several or many years, and the same registry mark would apply. Also not all pieces manufactured from 1842 on had a registry mark of either kind. The registry numbers and marks are useful only as a clue to the *period* when the pattern or shape was first invented.

It is generally accepted that the word "England" (or any other country's name) in a mark indicates a date later than 1890. The McKinley Tariff Act of 1890 stated that goods imported to this country must be marked with a country of origin. However, some manufacturers used England (or whatever country) in their marks before that time. Also some pieces manufactured after that time might not be marked at all--for example, all pieces in a set of china. "Made in England" is considered to be a 20th century mark. The words "Trade Mark" and "Ltd." in English marks were not in use until after 1862.

Many English potteries at certain periods in their history devised their own methods and codes for dating their products. Copeland, Minton, Wedgwood, and Worcester are some examples. Detailed information on decoding these marks can be obtained from general books on marks also.

Perhaps the most common mistake in attributing English marked wares is when the mark includes the name "Wedgwood". Several companies used this name in their marks. All "Wedgwood marks do not refer to Josiah Wedgwood, founder, circa 1759, of the famous Wedgwood company. His marks are impressed or printed. He did not spell his name with an "e" (Wedgewood), nor did he use the initial "J" in his marks, or use the mark of "Wedgwood & Co". Godden states that a John Wedge Wood operated a pottery from 1841 to 1860 and used a mark that incorporated the name J. Wedgwood. He notes that an impressed WEDGWOOD alone or WEDGWOOD & CO. is probably that of Ralph Wedgwood, circa 1780 to 1800. The impressed WEDGWOOD can thus be confusing for Josiah Wedgwood did use such a mark. But, according to Godden, the ceramic body of pieces with this mark are not up to par with that of Josiah's company. Podmore, Walker, and Co., circa 1860 also used Wedgwood & Co. in their marks. The Wedgwood was for Enoch Wedgwood who was associated with the company. See Marks 50 through 54.

For the English marks shown in this book, I have included dates where possible. These dates indicate the time the mark was first used by a company or the time period during which the company used the mark. These dates are based on information from Geoffrey A. Godden's *Encyclopedia of British Pottery and Porcelain*, 1964. See this book for more detailed historical information of the English potteries.

Blue Willow of Japanese origin is largely from the 20th century. Ceramics are marked with different symbols and initials combined with or only marked "Japan", "Made in Japan", or "Made in Occupied Japan". It is not possible usually to say what particular company or potter the marks stand for. Sometimes we find that the marks are just for American importing companies. Thus it is difficult to date 20th century Japanese wares more precisely than certain time periods.

From 1891 to 1921, the word "Nippon" was used alone or with symbols to mark ceramic ware made in Japan for export. "Nippon" was the name the country was called during this period. Also "Made in Nippon" is sometimes seen. In 1921, "Nippon" was discontinued in marks to comply with United States customs laws which determined that the word "Nippon" would not suffice any longer to designate country of origin, and that the imported items must use "Japan" to designate the country. Thus, after September 1921 until c. 1940, and after 1953, "Made in Japan", or "Japan" was used to mark Japanese products. It is sometimes suggested that "Made in Japan" was only used from 1921 to 1940, and that "Japan" alone was only used after 1953. However, by comparing examples with these marks, it is evident that some items just marked "Japan" are older than some marked "Made in Japan", and some items marked "Made in Japan" appear to be later than 1940. After World War II, from c. 1948 to 1953, "Occupied Japan", or "Made in Occupied Japan", was included with Japanese marks or used alone to designate that Japan was occupied by a foreign country. Due to the short time period this type of mark was used, items so marked are often higher in price than other wares of Japanese origin. Paper labels were used from the Nippon era to the present to denote country of origin on Japanese goods. Because they are easily removable, many Japanese items must be relegated to the "unmarked" category.

We find that the first Blue Willow pattern produced in the United States was by the Buffalo Pottery Company of Buffalo, New York, in 1905. After that time many other American potteries produced Blue Willow items. But it is important to remember that American examples of Blue Willow do not date prior to 1905 even though the particular pottery many have been in business many or several years before the Buffalo Pottery first perfected the underglaze Blue Willow pattern. Some American companies such as Buffalo Pottery (and Buffalo China) and Homer Laughlin did use dates or letters and numbers in some of their marks to indicate when pieces were made. However, that is not the rule for the majority of companies. References on American potters do give information as to the beginning and closing dates of the firms, but rarely do they give exact dates or time periods for the various marks each company used. To avoid any misunderstanding for American marks, I show only closing dates (where known) for the American companies' marks that are illustrated here because it might be interpreted that the Blue Willow piece with that mark was made, say in 1879, if the company began operations in that year. The piece itself may help you to know whether it was manufactured in the 1920's, 1950's, or 1980's. For more detailed information concerning American potters, see Edwin A. Barber's *Marks of American Potters*, 1976, and Lois Lehner's *Ohio Pottery and Glass*, 1978.

COLLECTING BLUE WILLOW

Just as there is not one Blue Willow legend or one Blue Willow pattern, there is not just one category of Blue Willow Collector. Some collect only the old while others collect not just for age but for type of item as well. Some concentrate on English or American examples. Some prefer one particular company's pattern while others are interested in acquiring examples of as many different makers' marks as possible.

Due to the pattern's long history, one finds examples dating from many different time periods. English pieces from the early 1800's (some of which are in museums) to 1880 are classified as true antiques as they are over a hundred years old. Many examples from the latter part of this period are available for collectors. Numerous items manufactured in countries other than England, such as Japan and the United States during the latter part of the 19th century and early 20th century, are fast approaching this "antique" status. Additionally, pieces dating from the 1930's to 1950's are definitely considered collectable as well as more recent items from the 1960's and 1970's that are collected due to their uniqueness or scarcity. One can say that this field of collecting has something for everyone ranging from antique to modern and from inexpensive knick knacks to articles of museum quality.

Blue Willow items show not only a variation in type of object but also a variation in quality. The quality depends on the type of ceramic body and the particular manufacturer. Concerning ceramic body, hard paste porcelain and bone china are the most exquisite in appearance as they are translucent and light in weight, but also durable. Ironstone and stoneware are quite durable but are heavy in texture and appearance. Semi-porcelain is the least durable for it is fired at lower temperatures than porcelain and stoneware. Earthenwares break more easily and they also are subject to crazing because they are not fired at high enough temperatures to fuse the body and the glaze. Glazes on earthenwares vary from thin and easily scratched to glossy and impenetrable. The majority of Blue Willow items are earthenwares. However, depending on the manufacturer, and the time period when the pieces were manufactured, some earthenwares are of fine quality with first rate decoration and color while some porcelain examples may have poor decoration. Transfer designs range on all classes of ceramic bodies from beautifully clear and distinct to faint or smudged. (See Plate 172 for example.) Because of this variation in workmanship, collectors learn to be choosy and consider the quality of the overall piece as well as the particular item when adding to their collection.

Other important facets for collectors of Blue Willow are examples of the Willow pattern in colors other than blue or multi-colored patterns. During the first quarter of the 19th century, transfer designs in other colors were tried and eventually perfected. Black, brown, and mulberry were among the first that met with success. From the turn of this century to the present, we find that the Willow pattern has been made in practically every color.

The multi-colored or polychromed willow items are quite striking in appearance. In the early days, the different colors were applied by hand over the glaze to the underglaze Blue Willow pattern. The Buffalo Pottery in the United States was not only the first American company to produce a Blue Willow pattern underglaze, but it was also the first to have a multi-colored version. As technology increased, it was possible to make multi-colored patterns under the glaze as well. Some examples of the pattern in other colors and multi-colors are shown in the photographs.

Historically, Blue Willow items have been inexpensive. From the late 1800's to the present, Blue Willow items have been sold through catalog ordering companies, variety stores, and even given as premiums with certain products. Pricewise, today we find that the handpainted multi-colored pieces and early examples in other solid colors are the most expensive. For standard Blue Willow tableware items, those of English origin are more costly than similar Japanese and American ones. In most fields of collection, the older the pieces, the higher the prices. However, as noted earlier, because willow collecting encompasses such a broad time period together with a stable popularity of the pattern that makes new items as equally acceptable by many collectors as the old, this rule of thumb does not always hold true. Many modern items may cost as much or more than the genuinely old ones. In fact, in the past collectors have often been able to purchase really rare, old, and unusual items for quite small sums. But as collector interest increases and sellers become more knowledgeable, prices escalate for these kinds of pieces. This is quite apparent from current prices on Blue Willow items seen at shops and shows. In fact, it has only been within the last few years that very much Blue Willow has been seen at antique shows. If the quality of the piece is good, if it is old, or if it is unusual, the item should command a premium. Cake stands, cheese dishes, cruet sets, infant feeders, mustard pots, and wash sets are just a few of such items pictured here. Take a careful look at these Blue Willow treasures so that you won't pass up a real "find"!

HAPPY BLUE WILLOWING!

MARKS

The majority of marks shown are found on pieces illustrated in this book. In each description of a piece, I indicate the mark, where known, using the numbers of the marks shown here. If the mark is known but not shown, the information is included in the photograph's caption. The marks are numbered consecutively and are arrranged alphabetically by country of origin and alphabetically within country by name of company. I have also included some other marks found on Blue Willow plates which do not have a corresponding photograph.

For convenience and not to be repetitive in the photograph captions, the following numbers correspond to marks for the different countries:

Mark Number	Country
1	Belgium
2-63	England
64	Finland
65-69	France
70	Germany
71-72	Holland
73	Ireland
74-99	Japan
100	Mexico
101	Poland
102-104	Scotland
105	Sweden
106-144	United States

MARK 1. Manufacture Imperial Royale, Nimy

MARK 2. W.A. Adderly, c. 1876 to 1885

MARK 3. Probably John and George Alcock, c. 1839 to 1846

MARK 4. Charles Allerton and Sons, c. 1890

MARK 5. Charles Allerton and Sons, c. 1890 to 1912

MARK 6. Charles Allerton and Sons, c. 1903 to 1912

MARK 9. Booths, c. 1912

MARK 7. Charles Allerton and Sons, c. 1929 to 1942

MARK 8. G.L. Ashworth, c. 1880

MARK 11. Burgess and Leigh, c. 1930's

MARK 12. Burgess and Leigh, c. 1930's

MARK 10. Sampson Bridgwood, c. 1885

MARK 13. Burgess and Leigh, Modern

MARK 14. Coalport, c. 1960

MARK 15. Copeland and Garrett, c. 1843 to 1847

MARK 16. W.T. Copeland and Sons, c. 1883

MARK 17. W.T. Copeland, c. 1875 to 1890

MARK 18. Crown Staffordshire Porcelain Company, Ltd., c. 1930 to 1947

MARK 19. Doulton & Co., Ltd., c. 1882 to 1890

MARK 20. Doulton & Co., Ltd., c. 1891 to 1902

MARK 21. Doulton & Co., Ltd., after 1891 to c. 1902

MARK 22. Royal Doulton, c. 1902 without "Made in England", after 1930 with "Made in England".

MARK 23. Dudson, Wilcox, & Till, Ltd., c. 1902 to 1926

MARK 24. Edge, Malkin, and Co., Ltd., c. 1873 to 1903

MARK 25. Furnivals, c. 1905 to 1913

MARK 26. Gater, Hall & Co., after 1914

MARK 27. T.G. Green and Co., c. 1892

MARK 28. Sampson Hancock and Sons, c. 1912 to 1937

MARK 29. Probably Hackwood and Keeling, c. 1835 to 1836

MARK 30. Johnson Bros., after 1912

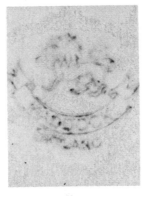

MARK 31. Probably Keeling and Co., c. 1840 to 1850

MARK 32. John Maddock, c. 1961

MARK 33. C.T. Maling, c. 1875 to 1908

MARK 34. Masons, after 1891

MARK 35. Masons, after 1891

MARK 36. Miles Mason, c. 1800 to 1816

MARK 37. W.R. Midwinter, c. 1946

MARK 38. Alfred Meakin, after 1930

MARK 39. Myott, Son, and Co., c. 1936

MARK 40. N & B., before 1891, company not identified

MARK 41. Palissy Pottery Ltd., c. 1908 to 1936

MARK 42. Parrott and Co., c. 1935

MARK 43. Pountney & Co., Ltd., after 1900

MARK 44. Samuel Radford, Ltd., c. mid 1920's

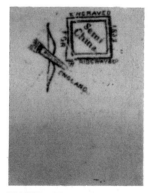

MARK 45. Ridgways, c. 1927; Bow and Quiver mark alone, c. 1912 to 1927

MARK 46. Ridgways, c. 1927, in red

MARK 47. Royal Staffordshire Pottery, c. 1907

MARK 48. John Steventon and Sons, Ltd., c. 1923 to 1936

MARK 49. George Townsend, c. 1850 to 1864

MARK 50. Wedgwood & Co., after 1891

MARK 51. Wedgwood & Co., c. 1908

MARK 53. Josiah Wedgwood, after 1891

MARK 52. Josiah Wedgwood, c. 1878

MARK 54. Josiah Wedgwood, Modern

MARK 57. Wood and Sons, Ltd.

MARK 55. Wood and Sons, Ltd., c. 1910

MARK 56. Wood and Sons, Ltd., c. 1917

MARK 58. Wood and Sons, Ltd., c. 1960

MARK 59. Worcester Royal Porcelain Co., c. 1882

MARK 60. Unidentified company, before 1891

MARK 62. Unidentified company

MARK 63. Unidentified company

MARK 61. Unidentified company

MARK 64. Arabia, Helsinki, after 1948

MARK 65. Grands Establissements Ceramique, Nord, before 1891

MARK 66. Hamage and Moulin des Loups, Nord, after 1891

MARK 69. Unidentified company, 20th century

MARK 67. Keller and Guerin, Luneville, after 1891

MARK 68. Unidentified company, after 1891

MARK 70. Villeroy and Bock, 20th century

MARK 71. Petrus Regout, before 1891

MARK 72. Societe Cerami- que, after 1891

2-Grill Plates

24

MARK 73. Arklow, Modern

MARK 74. Royal Sometuke, Nippon, c. 1891 to 1921

MARK 75. H.B., Made in Japan

MARK 76. House of Blue Willow, Made in Japan

MARK 77. M.D., Made in Japan

MARK 78. Mopiyama, Made in Japan

MARK 79. Noritake, Made in Japan after 1904

MARK 80. S.P.M.C., Made in Japan

MARK 81. Y.S., Made in Japan

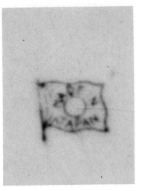

MARK 82. No initials, wreath mark, Made in Japan

MARK 83. No initials, flag, Made in Japan

MARK 84. No initials, crown, Made in Japan

MARK 85. No initials, tulips, Made in Japan

MARK 86. Kakusa China, Made in Occupied Japan

MARK 87. Morikin Ware, Made in Occupied Japan

MARK 88. N.K. Porcelain Co., Made in Occupied Japan

MARK 89. No initials, crown, Made in Occupied Japan

MARK 90. R.P., Made in Occupied Japan

MARK 91. Appears to Be N.K., Made in Occupied Japan

MARK 92. No initials, wreath and flower, Made in Japan, Occupide

MARK 93. Heirloom, Japan

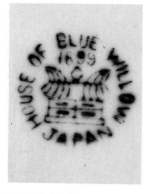

MARK 94. House of Blue Willow, Japan

MARK 95. Grantcrest, Japan

MARK 96. N. K. Porcelain Co.

MARK 97. Old Tower, Japan

MARK 98. Royal M by Nikko, Japan

MARK 99. Transor Ware, Japan

MARK 100. Anfora, Modern

MARK 101. Unidentified

MARK 102. J. and M.P. Bell and Co., c. 1842 to 1881

MARK 103. Britannia Pottery Co., Ltd., c. 1920 to 1935 (with Scotland)

MARK 104. Britannia Pottery Co., Ltd., c. 1920 to 1935 (with Gr. Britain)

MARK 105. Old Gustavsberg

MARK 106. The Bailey-Walker Co., Bedford, Ohio, the older mark of Walker China Company

MARK 107. Bennett, Baltimore, Maryland

MARK 108. Buffalo Pottery, Buffalo, New York, c. 1905 to 1915

MARK 109. Buffalo China, Buffalo, New York, after 1915

MARK 110. Carr China, Grafton, West Virginia

MARK 111. Cleveland China, Cleveland, Ohio, before 1950

MARK 114. Homer Laughlin, mark for June, 1964

MARK 112. Homer Laughlin, East Liverpool, Ohio, company currently in operation

MARK 113. Homer Laughlin

MARK 115. Hamilton Ross Ming Red Dinnerware, company not identified

MARK 116. Company not identified

MARK 117. Jackson China, Falls Creek, Pennsylvania

MARK 118. Jackson China

MARK 119. Knickerbocker, company unidentified

MARK 120. Edwin M. Knowles, East Liverpool, Ohio, before 1963

MARK 121. Limoges, Sebring, Ohio, before 1955

MARK 122. Limoges, Sebring, Ohio, before 1955

MARK 123. Nelson McCoy, Roseville, Ohio, currently in production

MARK 124. McNicol China, Clarksburg, West Virginia

MARK 125. Mayer China, Beaver Falls, Pennsylvania

MARK 126. The Paden City Pottery, Paden City, West Virginia

MARK 127. Royal China Company, Sebring, Ohio, currently in production

MARK 128. Royal China Company

MARK 129. Royal China Company

MARK 132. Sebring Pottery Company, Sebring, Ohio, before 1935

MARK 130. Royal China Company

MARK 131. E.H. Sebring, Sebring, Ohio, before 1935

MARK 134. Sterling China Company, East Liverpool, Ohio (offices), currently in production

MARK 133. Sebring Pottery Company, Sebring, Ohio, before 1935

MARK 135. Sterling China Company

31

MARK 136. Sterling China
Company

MARK 137. Shenango
China, New Castle,
Pennsylvania

MARK 138. Shenango
China

MARK 139. Company not
identified

MARK 140. Walker China
Company, Bedford, Ohio,
currently in production

MARK 141. Walker China
Company, currently in
production

MARK 142. Wallace China
Company, Vernon, California

MARK 143. Wallace China
Company

MARK 144. Wellsville
China, Wellsville, Ohio,
before 1970

PLATE 1. Advertising Coaster, 4½″d., Mark 67. $12.00-15.00.

Keller & Guerin After 1912

PLATE 2. Advertising Coaster, 4″d., English, unmarked. $12.00-15.00.

PLATE 3. Ash Tray, 6″sq., Mark 22. $20.00-25.00.

PLATE 4. Auld Lang Syne Cup, Marked "Copeland's China, England." $25.00-30.00.

PLATE 5. Baking Dish, Oven Proof, 2½"h., 5"d., Marked "Japan". $12.00-15.00.

PLATE 6. Baking Dish, 3"h., 8"d., American, Marked "Hall China". $12.00-15.00.

PLATE 7. Bathroom Cup, 3½″h.,
Mark 11. $16.00-20.00.

Burgess Leigh 1920

PLATE 8. Batter Jug, 8½″h., Frosted
glass, should have syrup type lid,
marked "H A" in monogram for Hazel
Atlas Company, United States.
$20.00-25.00.

PLATE 9. Bone Dish, 7½″l., 4½″w., Mark 58. $15.00-18.00.

Wood & Sons   1960

PLATE 10. Bone Dish (Turkey bones). 8¼″l., English, "Minton" impressed mark for February 1878, Dagger Border. $30.00-35.00.

PLATE 11. Bread Bowl, 15″d., unmarked. $100.00-125.00.

PLATE 12. Bread Tray, 12″l., Mark 9. $80.00-90.00.

Booth's 1912

38

PLATE 13. Butter Dish, 7″l., 4½″w., Japanese, unmarked. $20.00-25.00.

Myott & Son 1938

PLATE 14. Butter Dish, Mark 39. $65.00-75.00.

Myott & Son 1938

PLATE 15. Butter Dish, 7½″d., Mark 6. $75.00-85.00.

Allerton's 1903 -1912

PLATE 16. Butter Dish, 8″d., Mark 109. $60.00-70.00.

Buffalo China 1909

PLATE 17. Butter Pats, from top and left to right: 3″, Mark 39; 3″, unmarked, $10.00-12.00; 3½″, England; 3½″, England; 3″, "Made in Japan", $12.00-15.00; 3″, England, $15.00-20.00.

PLATE 18. Butter Warmer, unmarked. $18.00-22.00.

Top Only

41

PLATE 19. Cake Plate, 10″sq., Flow Blue, English, marked "Balmoral China", over Lion, company initials illegible. $30.00-35.00.

PLATE 20. Cake Plate, 10″d., Mark 7. $30.00-35.00.

PLATE 21. Cake Stand, 3"h., 12"d., Mark 40. $125.00-150.00.

M&B Stone Chine (Before 1941)

PLATE 22. Cake Stand, 2½"h., 8½"d., English, unmarked. $100.00-125.00.

PLATE 23. Cake Stand, 2″h., 10½″d., English, unmarked. $125.00-150.00.

PLATE 24. Candelabra, 11″h., with matching side dishes, brass, unmarked.
$80.00-90.00 set.

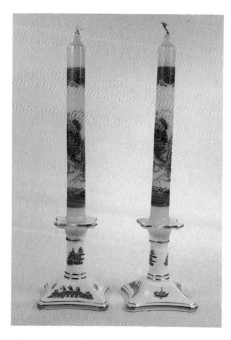

PLATE 25. Candle Holders (and Blue Willow Candles), 5½″h., 3″sq. base, Mark 14. $100.00-110.00.

Coal port 1960

PLATE 26. Candle Holders, 7½″h., Flow Blue, Mark 20. $250.00-275.00.

DaltonCo, 1891-1902

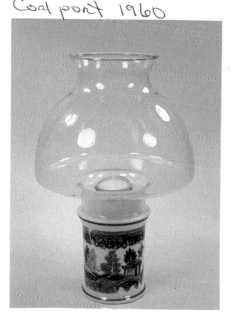

PLATE 27. Candle Lamp, 11½″h., Modern. $15.00-20.00.

PLATE 28. Candle Ship's Light, unmarked. $40.00-50.00.

PLATE 29. Candle Stand,
4½"h., 5"d., Modern.
$20.00-25.00.

PLATE 30. Candle Snuffer, 2½"h., Mark 14, Modern. $25.00-30.00.

PLATE 31. Cannisters, 10½"h., 9½"h., 8½"h, Japanese. $60.00-80.00.

PLATE 32. Cannisters, 8½"h., 6"h., 5"h., unmarked. $80.00-100.00.

PLATE 33. Carafe and Warmer, 10″h. overall, Marked "Japan". $125.00-150.00.

PLATE 34. Charger, 13″d., Mark 7. $35.00-45.00.

PLATE 35. Cheese Dish, unmarked. $80.00-100.00.

PLATE 36. Children's Toy Dishes: Grill Plate, 4½"d., $8.00-10.00; Cake Plate,
5"d., Marked "Made in Japan", $10.00-12.00; Tin Plate, 1½"d., unmarked,
$5.00-8.00.

PLATE 37. Children's Toys Dishes (porcelain): Plate, 5½"d.; Soup, 3½"d.; Cup, 1½"h.; Gravy, 2½"h., 5"l.; Sugar, 3½"h.; Creamer, 3"h.; Teapot, 4½"h.; Oval Vegetable Dish, 5½"l.; Covered Vegetable Dish, 3½"h., 5½"d.; Platter, 7"l., 4½"d., Marked "Made in Japan". $200.00-225.00 set.

PLATE 38. Chili Cup, 4"h., 4¼"d., unmarked. $15.00-18.00

PLATE 39. Clock, 8 Day, German Works, Tin. $70.00-80.00.

PLATE 40. Clock Marked "Smith's, Made in Great Britain". $70.00-80.00.

PLATE 41. Coffee Cans, 2¼″h., 2½″h., English, unmarked. $15.00-18.00.

PLATE 42. Coffee Cup, Red Willow, c. 1900, unmarked. $20.00-25.00.

PLATE 43. Coffee or Tea Cup and Saucer, Mark 133. Simple Line Border, Two Temples II Simplified Center. $10.00-12.00.

Sebring Pottery - Before 1935

PLATE 44. Coffee or Tea Cup and Saucer, Black Willow, English, unmarked. $30.00-35.00.

PLATE 45. Coffee or Tea Cup and Saucer, Mark 73. $15.00-20.00.

PLATE 46. Coffee Pot, 9"h., Mark 30. $50.00-60.00.

Johnson Bros After 1912

PLATE 47. Coffee Pot, 8″h., Mark 54, Modern $70.00-80.00.

Josiah Wedgwood Modern

PLATE 48. Compote, 5″h., 9½″d., Mark 14. $140.00-150.00.

Coalport 1960

PLATE 49. Compote, 3″h., 9½″d., Unmarked, Simple Line Border, Simplified Pattern, Polychromed. $55.00-65.00.

PLATE 50. Compote, 3″h., 9″d., Flow Blue, Mark 21. $130.00-150.00.

Doulton & Co. 1891-902.

PLATE 51. Compote, 3″h., 5½″d., American, made by Cambridge Glass, Cambridge, Ohio, c. 1920's, unmarked. $40.00-50.00.

PLATE 52. Cook Ware (includes 10″ Skillet not shown), General Housewares, Modern. $100.00-125.00.

PLATE 53. Cream Soup, 7″d., Mark 74, $15.00-18.00; Bread and Butter, 6½″d. (in back), Mark 79, Pictorial Borders. $10.00-12.00.

Noritake-Japan After 1904

PLATE 54. Cream soup, Cup, 2½″h., Saucer, 6″d., Mark 45. $30.00-35.00.

Ridgeways 1912-1927

PLATE 55. Creamer, 4″h., Sugar, 4″h., 7″ across, Mark 7. $75.00-85.00.

Allerton's 1929-1942

PLATE 56. Creamer, 4″h., Sugar, 5″h., Mark 9. $80.00-90.00.

Booth's 1912 (England)

59

PLATE 57. Creamers, front to back: 2¼″, Maddock, England; 2″, unmarked, bisque; 2½″, Buffalo China, American; 2¼″, Buffalo China, American; 2″, Walker China, American; 3″ Shenango, American; 1½″, Shenango, American. $12.00-16.00 each.

PLATE 58. Crisper, 10″h., Marked "Blue Magic Krispy Kan, The Luce Corp., South Norwalk, Conn.". $8.00-10.00.

PLATE 59. Cruet Set, 7½"h. overall, Marked "Japan". $150.00-175.00

PLATE 60. Demi-tasse Cup, 2½"h., Saucer, 5"d., Mark 9. $20.00-25.00.

Booth's 1912 (England)

PLATE 61. Demi-tasse Cup,
2½″h., Saucer, 4½″d., Mark
30. $16.00-20.00.

Johnson Bros. after 1913

PLATE 62. Demi-tasse Cup, 2½″h., Saucer, 5″d., unmarked, Butterfly Border,
Two Temples II Center. $12.00-15.00.

PLATE 63. Demi-tasse Cup, 2½″h., Saucer, 5½″d., unmarked, Dagger Border, Mandarin II center. $16.00-20.00.

PLATE 64. Demi-tasse Cup, 2½″h., Mark 64. $10.00-12.00.

PLATE 65. Demi-tasse Cup, 2½"h., Saucer, 4½"d., Mark 13. $15.00-18.00.

PLATE 66. Demi-tasse Cup, 2½"h., Saucer 4½"d., English, Marked "Copeland". Dagger Border, Mandarin II Center. $20.00-25.00.

PLATE 67. Demi-tasse Pot, 7½"h., Mark 11, Scroll and Flower Border, Burleigh Pattern. $80.00-90.00.

PLATE 68. Dresser set: Tray, 12"l., 7½"w. $75.00-80.00; Pin tray, 5¼"l., 3¼"w. $20.00-25.00; Open Jar, 3¼"h., Mark 22. $25.00-30.00.

PLATE 69. Drainers: Butter, 3½″d., $20.00-25.00; and 4″sq., $20.00-25.00; Meat, 6″sq., $25.00-30.00; unmarked, English.

PLATE 70. Drainer, Meat, 14¼″l., 10¼″w., English, unmarked, Turner Center Pattern. $70.00-80.00.

PLATE 71. Drainer, Meat, 10″l., 7¼″w., English, Marked "Iron Stone China".
$40.00-50.00.

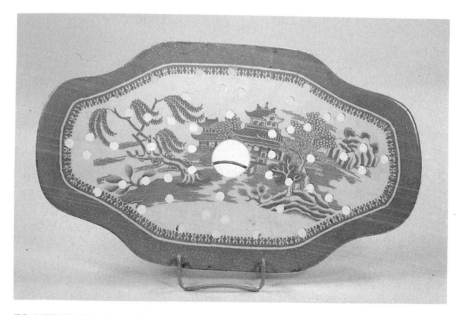

PLATE 72. Drainer, Meat, 16″l., Dagger Border. $70.00-80.00.

PLATE 73. Egg, 5½"l., Japanese, Jewel or Trinket Box $70.00-80.00; Egg with Dove, 1½"l., Mark 14. $25.00-30.00.

PLATE 74. Egg cup, single type, English, unmarked. $16.00-18.00.

PLATE 75. Egg Cups, single type: left, 2½"h., Buffalo China Script mark: right, Mark 57. $18.00-20.00 each.

PLATE 76. Egg Cups: double type, 4"h. $15.00-18.00; single type, 2"h., unmarked. $10.00-12.00 each.

✗ PLATE 77. Egg Cups, double type: 3½″h., 4″h., Japanese, $15.00-18.00; 3½″h., Mark 7. $18.00-20.00.

2 - Similan - Japaan

PLATE 78. Egg Cups, double type: 3½″h., unmarked, $15.00-18.00; 4″h., Mark 9, $18.00-20.00; 3½″h, unmarked. $15.00-18.00.

PLATE 79. Farmers' Cups, 4"h., Marked "Japan". $10.00-12.00 each.

PLATE 80. Fish Plate, 10"l., 7"w., Mark 3, Mandarin II Center. $80.00-100.00.

PLATE 81. Ginger Jar, 7½″h., Mark 34, Scroll and Flower Border, Turner Pattern. $60.00-70.00.

PLATE 82. Ginger Jar, 9″h., Mark 35, Scroll and Flower Border, Turner Pattern. $60.00-70.00.

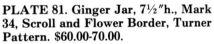

PLATE 83. Glass Plate, 9½″d., unmarked. $15.00-18.00.

PLATE 84. Glass Stemware, by Fostoria, c. early 1940's, American. $20.00-25.00 each.

PLATE 85. Glass, Pitcher, 10"h., $20.00-25.00; Glasses, 8"h., carnival-type glass. $8.00-10.00 each.

PLATE 86. Glass, Salad Plate, 8"d., $15.00-18.00, Cup, 2½"h, Saucer, 6"d., $16.00-20.00, and Bread and Butter, 6"d. (not shown), $12.00-15.00, by Cambridge Glass, Cambridge, Ohio, unmarked. Reversed Traditional Border and Center.

PLATE 87. Gravy, 2½″h., 6″l., Mark 23. $35.00-45.00.

PLATE 88. Gravy, 8″l., 4″h., Underplate, 9″l., 5″w., Mark 7. $50.00-60.00.

PLATE 89. Gravy, 3½"h., 8"l., English, "Copeland" impressed mark for 1882. Dagger Border inside and Mandarin II pattern on body. $60.00-70.00.

PLATE 90. Gravy, 4"h., 8½"l., Mark 9. $60.00-70.00.

PLATE 92. Honey Dish, 4″d., Mark 37. $12.00-16.00.

PLATE 91. Handleless Cup, 2½″h., English, unmarked. $30.00-40.00.

PLATE 93. Horseradish Dish, 5½″h., Mark 22. $25.00-30.00.

PLATE 94. Infant Feeder, 4″h., English, unmarked. $110.00-125.00.

PLATE 95. Instant Coffee Jar, 6″h.,
Marked "Japan". $15.00-20.00.

PLATE 96. Instant Coffee Jar with
plastic spoon measure, 6″h., unmarked. $15.00-20.00.

PLATE 97. Instant Coffee Jar, unmarked. $15.00-20.00.

PLATE 98. Juice Glasses, 3½″h., Japanese, unmarked. $8.00-10.00.

PLATE 99. Juice Glasses, 3½″h., Marked "Japan". $10.00-12.00.

78

PLATE 100. Juice Glasses, 4"h., unmarked, Modern. $10.00-12.00.

PLATE 101. Juice Set, Pitcher, 8½"h., Glasses, 3½"h., Japanese. $40.00-50.00 set.

PLATE 102. Juice Set, Pitcher, 10″h., Glasses, 5″h., unmarked, Modern. $50.00-60.00 set.

PLATE 103. Juicer, decal decoration, Japanese, Modern. $10.00-15.00.

PLATE 104. Lamp, Kerosene with Reflector, 8"h., Japanese. $50.00-55.00.

PLATE 105. Lamp made from Teapot, English, Butterfly Border, Two Temples II pattern on body. $45.00-50.00.

PLATE 106. Lamps, Kerosene: 8"h., $35.00-40.00; 8½"h., $40.00-45.00; 11½"h., Japanese. $45.00-50.00.

PLATE 107. Lamp Base, 10″h., one of a pair, Mulberry Willow, marked "Made in England". $165.00-185.00 pair.

PLATE 108. Match Safe, 2″h., Mark 138. $25.00-35.00.

PLATE 109. Milk Glass, Plate, 11½"d., American, by Kemple Glass, East Palestine, Ohio; Borderless, Two Temples Variant Simplified Reversed Center. $20.00-25.00.

PLATE 110. Milk Glass, Plate, 10"d., unmarked, Simple Line Border, Simplified Center. $16.00-20.00.

PLATE 111. Milk Pitcher, marked "Keele Pottery, England," c. 1913 to 1945, Two Temples II Simplified pattern on body, Polychromed. $65.00-75.00.

PLATE 112. Milk Pitcher, 4"h., Mark 27, Polychromed. $80.00-100.00.

PLATE 113. Milk Pitcher, 5½"h., Mark 58. $40.00-45.00.

PLATE 114. Milk Pitcher, 9"h., Mark 123. $25.00-30.00.

PLATE 115. Milk Pitcher, 12″h., English, unmarked, Polychromed. $125.00-145.00.

PLATE 116. Back of Plate 115.

PLATE 117. Milk Pitcher, 8″h., English, unmarked, Pictorial Border, Two Temples II Simplified pattern on body. $90.00-100.00.

PLATE 118. Back of Plate 117.

PLATE 119. Milk Pitcher, pewter lid, 7½″h., Mark 26, Polychromed, hand-painted. $140.00-160.00.

PLATE 120. Milk Pitcher, 5″h., Mark 24, Dagger Border, Mandarin II pattern. $50.00-55.00.

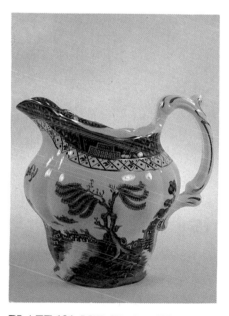

PLATE 122. Milk Pitcher, 5″h., Mark 34, Scroll and Flower Border, Turner pattern on body, Polychromed. $40.00-50.00.

PLATE 121. Milk Pitcher, 7″h., Mark 9. $50.00-60.00.

PLATE 123. Milk Pitchers: 6″h.; 5½″h., Mark 7. $50.00-55.00.

PLATE 124. Milk Pitchers: 4″h.; 4½″h., Mark 20. $55.00-65.00.

PLATE 125. Miniatures by Coalport: Cup, 1″h.; Saucer, 2½″d.; Plate, 3″d., $40.00-50.00; Thimble, 1″h., $15.00-20.00; Bell, 2″h., $20.00-25.00; Mark 14.

PLATE 126. Mustard Jar, 3½″h., Mark 42, Pictorial Border, Two Temples II Simplified pattern on body, Polychromed. $80.00-90.00.

PLATE 127. Mustard Jar with attached underplate, 3″h., unmarked. $45.00-55.00.

PLATE 128. Mustard Jar on left, 3½″h., $50.00-60.00; Toothpick Holder, 2½″h., $25.00-30.00, English.

PLATE 129. Napkin Plate, 6½"sq., Butterfly Border, Two Temples II Center, Mark 10. $45.00-55.00.

PLATE 130. Oil and Vinegar Set, 6"h., Japanese. $20.00-25.00 set.

PLATE 131. Pen Staff, Marked "H. & R. Johnson, Ltd., Made in England".
$20.00-25.00.

PLATE 132. Perfume Bottle and Stopper, 6"h., marked "Copeland", English.
$120.00-140.00.

PLATE 133. Pie Server, 10"l., Mark 78. $15.00-18.00.

PLATE 134. Piggy Bank, 7"h., Japanese, Modern. $20.00-25.00.

PLATE 136. Place Setting, flatware, Japanese. $15.00-18.00 place setting.

PLATE 135. Place Card Holder, 3"h., 2½"d., English, unmarked. $60.00-75.00.

PLATE 137. Place Setting, Mark 9, Booth's Pattern (Butterfly Border). Plate, $20.00-25.00; Cup/Saucer, $22.00-26.00.

PLATE 138. Place Setting, Mark 9, Salad, $16.00-20.00; Bread & Butter, $12.00-15.00; Fruit, $10.00-12.00.

PLATE 139. Place Setting, Mark 7 except Butter Pat is Mark 4, Traditional Border and Center, Plate, $18.00-20.00; Soup, $18.00-22.00; Luncheon Plate, $16.00-20.00; Salad, $12.00-15.00; Bread & Butter, $10.00-12.00; Butter Pat, $12.00-15.00; Fruit, $8.00-10.00; Cereal, $12.00-15.00; Large Cup/Saucer, $20.00-23.00; Small Cup/Saucer, $18.00-20.00.

PLATE 140. Planter, 6"h., American. $12.00-15.00.

PLATE 141. Grill Plates, 10″d., Mark 1. $14.00-18.00.

PLATE 142. Plate, 10″d., Chinese, handpainted "Canton" pattern. $60.00-70.00.

PLATE 143. Plate, 8½″d., Mark 2, Adderly's "Daisy" pattern, Floral Border. $35.00-45.00.

PLATE 144. Plate, 10″d., Mark 7, Traditional Border and Center. $16.00-20.00.

PLATE 145. Plate, 9″d., Mark 4, Butterfly Border, Two Temples II Center. $20.00-25.00.

PLATE 146. Plate, 7½″d., Mark 5, Butterfly Border, Two Temples II Center. $15.00-20.00.

PLATE 147. Plate, 9½″d., Mark 14, Bicentenary Plate. $45.00-55.00.

PLATE 148. Back of Bicentenary Plate.

PLATE 149. Plate, 8½″d., English, "Copeland" impressed mark for 1879, Dagger Border, Mandarin II Center. $20.00-25.00.

PLATE 150. Plate, 9″d., English, "Copeland" impressed mark for 1883, Dagger Border, Mandarin II Center. $20.00-25.00.

PLATE 151. Plate, 9″d., Octagonal shape, Mark 15, Butterfly Border Two Temples I Center. Note Border variation from Two Temples II Butterfly Border (see Plate 159). $30.00-35.00.

PLATE 152. Plate, 9″d., Mark 18, Butterfly Border, Two Temples II Variation Center (note presence of birds), Polychromed. $40.00-50.00.

PLATE 153. Plate, 9½″d., Mark 19, Flow Blue, Traditional Border and Center. $50.00-60.00.

PLATE 154. Plate, 8½″d., Mark 19 with "Made in England", Brown Glaze, Traditional Border and Center. $40.00-50.00.

PLATE 155. Plate, 10½"d., one of a series of plates relating the Willow Story, issued by Royal Doulton from 1920 to 1945. The center pattern portrays one part of the story (see Plate 156), with cameos around the border from the other plates in the series. $75.00-85.00.

PLATE 156. Description of center pattern in Plate 155.

PLATE 157. Plate, 9″d., Mark 25, Pattern name in Mark is "Hong Kong", Pictorial Border, no center pattern, Polychromed. $25.00-30.00.

PLATE 158. Plate, 9″d., "The Old York Willow Pattern," commemorative plate issued in 1978 for the Castle Museum, York, England by the Gladstone Pottery Museum, Longton, Stoke-on-Trent. $20.00-25.00.

PLATE 159. Plate, 9″d., Mark 29, Butterfly Border, Two Temples II Center. $15.00-20.00.

PLATE 160. Plate, 8½d., Mark 31, Butterfly Border, Two Temples II Center. $15.00-20.00.

PLATE 161. Plate, 10″d., Mark 32, Traditional Variant Border, Traditional Center, Polychromed. $20.00-25.00.

PLATE 162. Bowl, 6½″d., Mason's "Canton" Pattern, Mark 34. $12.00-15.00.

PLATE 163. Plate, 10″d., Mark 34, Scroll and Flower Border Turner Center. $15.00-18.00.

PLATE 164. Plate, 10″d., Mark 36, Butterfly Border, Two Temples I Center. $40.00-50.00.

PLATE 165. Plate, 10″d., Mark 38, Traditional Border and Center. $16.00-20.00.

PLATE 166. Plate, 10¼″d., Mark 41, Pictorial Border, Two Temples II Simplified Center. $20.00-25.00.

PLATE 167. Plate, 7¼″d., Flow Blue, Mark 43, name of pattern in mark is "Mandarin", but Border is Scroll and Flower and Center is Worcester. $25.00-30.00.

PLATE 168. Sauce Dish, 5″d., Mark 46, Butterfly Border, Two Temples II Center, Polychromed, handpainted. $20.00-25.00.

103

PLATE 169. Saucer, 5½"d., Mark 45, Butterfly Border, Two Temples II Center. $10.00-12.00.

PLATE 170. Plate, 6½"d., English, marked "Royal Alma", mark is after 1950. Dagger Variant Border, Traditional Center. $20.00-25.00.

PLATE 171. Plate, 9¼"d., Mark 47, Traditional Border and Center, Polychromed, (handpainted). $80.00-100.00.

PLATE 172. Plate, 10"d., Mark 49, $10.00-12.00; Plate, 8"d., Mark 44, $15.00-20.00; both have Traditional Borders and Centers. Note quality variation in transfer work.

PLATE 173. Plate, 8″d., Mark 50, Traditional Border and Center. $25.00-30.00.

PLATE 174. Plate, 6″d., Mark 53, Traditional Border and Center. $15.00-20.00.

PLATE 175. Plate, 9¼″d., Mark 52, Scroll and Flower Border, Traditional Center. $65.00-75.00.

PLATE 176. Plate, 7″d., Mark 54 (without "Willow"), Wedgwood Collector Plate issued in 1971 portraying a scene from "The Sandman", a fairy tale by Hans Christian Andersen. $20.00-25.00.

PLATE 177. Plate, 9″d., Mark 56, Wood's "Canton" pattern. $20.00-25.00.

PLATE 178. Plate, 7″d., Mark 59, Worcester pattern (Scroll and Flower Border). $25.00-30.00.

PLATE 179. Plate, 9″d., unmarked, handpainted," Canton" Pattern. $40.00-50.00.

PLATE 180. Plate, 6″d., unmarked, handpainted, Canton Variant Pattern. $30.00-40.00.

PLATE 181. Plate, 8½″d., Octagonal shape, English, porcelain, "Copeland" mark for 1883. Dagger Border, Mandarin II Center. $40.00-50.00.

PLATE 182. Plate, 10″d., unmarked, Traditional Border and Center. $15.00-18.00.

PLATE 183. Plate, 10″d., unmarked, porcelain, Butterfly Border, Two Temples II Center. $30.00-35.00.

PLATE 184. Plate, 9¼″d., Mark 68, Traditional Border and Center. $12.00-15.00.

PLATE 185. Plate, 9″d., Mark 66,
Traditional Border and Center.
$12.00-15.00.

PLATE 186. Plate, 9½d., Mark 70,
Traditional Border and Center.
$15.00-18.00.

PLATE 187. Plate, 10″d., Mark 72,
Traditional Border and Center.
$12.00-15.00.

PLATE 188. Plate, 9″d., Mark 71,
Traditional Border and Center.
$15.00-18.00.

PLATE 189. Plate, 10″d., Mark 98, Bow Knot Border, Two Phoenix Center (Japanese version and name for Booth's pattern). $15.00-18.00.

PLATE 190. Plate, 6½″d., Mark 96, Two Phoenix Center, note inner border variation in this example and that in Plate 189. $10.00-12.00.

PLATE 191. Grill Plate, 10″d., Marked, "Made in Occupied Japan", Traditional Border and Center. $12.00-15.00.

PLATE 192. Plate, 9¼″d., Two Phoenix Variation for center and border, marked "Japan". $12.00-14.00.

PLATE 193. Plate, 9¼"d., Traditional Variant Border and Center with 3 birds, unmarked. $10.00-12.00.

PLATE 194. Plate, 10"d., Mark 85. Traditional Border, Traditional Variant Center with 4 birds. $10.00-12.00.

PLATE 195. Plate, 10"d., Traditional Border and Center. $12.00-15.00.

PLATE 196. Plate, 9"d., Mark 100, Borderless, Simplified Center, $12.00-15.00; Cup has Traditional Border, $8.00-10.00.

PLATE 197. Grill Plate, 10½″d., Mark 101, Traditional Border, Traditional Variant Center. $15.00-18.00.

PLATE 198. Plate, 8½″d., Mark 105, Red Willow, Traditional Border and Center. $20.00-25.00.

PLATE 199. Restaurant Plate, 9″l., Mark 109 (1975), Traditional Border and Center. $12.00-15.00.

PLATE 200. Plate, 9½″d., Mark 108 (1911), Gaudy Willow, handpainted, Polychromed, Traditional Border and Center. $80.00-100.00.

PLATE 201. Plate, 9½"d,. Mark 109 (1912), Pink Willow, Traditional Border and Center. $20.00-25.00.

PLATE 202. Plate, 10"d., Mark 111, Borderless, Simplified Center, Polychromed. $12.00-15.00.

PLATE 203. Plate, 7″d., Mark 131, Pictorial Border, Simplified Center. $15.00-18.00.

PLATE 204. Plate, 5½″d., Mark 115, $5.00-8.00; Plate 6¼″, Mark 128, $8.00-10.00; both have Royal's Bridal Gold Floral Border pattern.

PLATE 205. Plate, 11″d., Mark 116, Scroll and Flower Border, Turner Center. $12.00-15.00.

PLATE 206. Plate, 10″d., Mark 120, Borderless, Simplified Center. $12.00-15.00.

PLATE 207. Plate, 9½″d., Mark 121, Simple Line Border, Simplified Center. $12.00-15.00.

PLATE 208. Plate, 10″d., Mark 122, Traditional Variant Border, Traditional Center. $12.00-15.00.

PLATE 209. Grill Plate, 9½″d., Mark 124, Traditional Border, Two Temples II Variation, Reversed. $12.00-15.00.

PLATE 210. Plate, 7½″d., Mark 126, Butterfly Border and Traditional Center, note that pattern is incised. $35.00-40.00.

PLATE 211. Plate, 10″d., Mark 130, Traditional Border and Center. $10.00-12.00.

PLATE 212. Grill Plate, 10″d., Mark 137, Scroll and Flower Border, Turner Center. $12.00-15.00.

PLATE 213. Plate, 11¼″d., American, Marked "Van, China", Trenton, New Jersey, Traditional Variant Border, Simplified Center. $12.00-15.00.

PLATE 214. Plate, 10″d., Mark 143, Brown Willow, Traditional Border and Center. $16.00-20.00.

PLATE 215. Grill Plate, 9½″d., Mark 142, Pink Willow, Traditional Border and Center. $16.00-20.00.

PLATE 216. Plate, 6¼d., marked "Wallace China", American (similar to Mark 142), Pictorial Border, Traditional Center. $12.00-15.00.

PLATE 217. Grill Plate, 10″d., Mark 144, Red Willow, Traditional Border and Center. $16.00-20.00.

PLATE 218. Grill Plate, 10¼″d., American, Traditional Border, Two Temples II Reversed Center, unmarked. $10.00-12.00.

PLATE 219. Platter, 7"l., 5½"w., (Bacon), Mark 7, Traditional Border and Center. $20.00-25.00.

PLATE 220. Platter, 11¼"l., 8½"w., Mark 11, Scroll and Flower Border, Burleigh Center. $60.00-75.00.

PLATE 221. Platter, 16"l., 14"w., Mark 9, Booth's Pattern (Bow Knot Border). $80.00-100.00.

PLATE 222. Platter, 11"l., 8½"w., English, "Copeland" incised mark for 1883, Dagger Border, Mandarin II Center. $50.00-60.00

PLATE 223. Platter, 11″l., 8″w., English, marked "Corona Ware, Stoke-on-Trent", Traditional Border Reversed, Traditional Center. $75.00-85.00

PLATE 224. Platter, Mark 45, Traditional Border and Center. $50.00-60.00.

PLATE 225. Platter, 6½"l., 5"w., (Bacon), Mark 46, Traditional Border and Center, Polychromed, handpainted. $45.00-55.00.

PLATE 226. Platter, 10¼"l., 7"w., Mark 53, Traditional Border and Center. $70.00-80.00.

PLATE 227. Platter, 19"l., 15½"w., Mark 60, scalloped footed base, Traditional Border and Center. $150.00-200.00.

PLATE 228. Platter, unmarked, Traditional Border and Center. $50.00-60.00.

PLATE 229. Platter, 11½″l., 9½″w., Mark 103, Mulberry Willow, Traditional Border and Center. $80.00-100.00; Covered Sugar 4½″h., 6″ across, Creamer 4½″h., Mark 104, $55.00-65.00 pair.

PLATE 230. Platter, 12″l., 10″w., Mark 102, Traditional Border and Center. $60.00-70.00.

PLATE 231. Pudding Mold, 3″h., Mark 9, Booth's pattern. $25.00-30.00.

PLATE 232. Pudding Mold, 3″h., 4½″d., unmarked, English, Pictorial Border, Two Temples II Simplified Center, Polychromed. $45.00-55.00.

PLATE 233. Pudding Mold, 4½″h., "England" incised mark. $30.00-35.00.

PLATE 234. Punch Bowl, 6″h., 9¼″d., unmarked. $115.00-130.00.

PLATE 235. Salad Bowl, square shape, 4″h., 9″d., Mark 45. $50.00-55.00.

PLATE 236. Salad Bowl, 3½″h., 10″d., fork and spoon. $30.00-40.00 set.

February 1983

PLATE 237. Salad Set, Fork and Spoon; Oil and Vinegar; Funnel, all on wooden wall-hanging rack, Japanese. $100.00-125.00.

PLATE 238. Salt Box, 5″h., 5″w., Japanese. $50.00-60.00.

PLATE 239. Open Salt, 2″h., 3″d., English, unmarked. $30.00-35.00.

PLATE 240. Salt and Pepper Shakers, 3″h., Japanese. $20.00-25.00.

PLATE 241. Salt and Pepper Shakers, 3″h., marked "JAPAN". $15.00-20.00.

PLATE 242. Salt and Pepper Shakers: 3″h., Japanese, $20.00-25.00; 3½″h., Japanese, $10.00-12.00 each; 3″h., unmarked, Modern, $25.00-30.00.

PLATE 243. Sauce Dish, 6″l., 3½″w., English, unmarked. $20.00-25.00.

PLATE 244. Scuttle Shaving Mug, 4″h., Mark 11. $45.00-55.00.

Burgess & Leigh 1930s

131

PLATE 245. Silver Plated Tray with Willow Pattern, 11½″d. $40.00-50.00.

PLATE 246. Soap Pad Holder, 6½″h.,
marked "JAPAN". $15.00-20.00.

PLATE 247. Soup Bowl, unmarked, English, Butterfly Border, Two Temples II Center. $30.00-35.00.

PLATE 248. Soup Spoon, 5½″l., Japanese. $4.00-6.00.

133

PLATE 249. Spice Set, Japanese. $40.00-50.00.

PLATE 250. Spoon Rest, 9″l., Japanese. $20.00-25.00.

PLATE 251. Sugar Shaker, 7"h., English, marked "Lancaster Ltd., Hanley, England", mark is after 1906, Polychromed. $90.00-110.00.

PLATE 252. Syrup Pitcher, 5"h., Frosted Glass. $25.00-30.00.

PLATE 253. Tea Caddy, 8"h., English, marked "Rington Limited, Tea Merchants, Newcastle upon Tyne"on base. $125.00-150.00.

PLATE 254. Tea Caddy, 8"h., same markings as in Plate 253, larger base. $125.00-150.00.

PLATE 256. Tea Kettle, unmarked, Modern. $35.00-40.00.

PLATE 255. Tea Caddy, Tin, English. $55.00-65.00.

PLATE 257. Teapot, 6½″h., 7″ across, $18.00-20.00; Mugs, 3¼″h., (set of 4), by General Housewares, Modern, $4.00-6.00 each; Tea Caddy (2 pieces), 3″h., Modern. $8.00-10.00.

PLATE 258. Tea Set: Teapot, Covered Sugar and Creamer, Mark 7. $150.00-175.00.

PLATE 259. Teapot, 6"h., Mark 8. $50.00-60.00.

PLATE 260. Teapot, 7″h., Mark 9, Booth's pattern. $65.00-75.00.

Booth -England - 1912

PLATE 261. Teapot, 5″h., 10″ across, $80.00-100.00; Trivet, 7½″d., Mark 12, Butterfly Border, Burleigh pattern on body and on Trivet. $30.00-35.00.

PLATE 262. Teapot, Mark 33, Mandarin II pattern on body. $60.00-70.00.

CT. Maling 1875 - 1908

PLATE 263. Teapot, 5½"h., 6¼" across, Mark 51. $55.00-65.00.

Wedgwood&Co 1905

PLATE 264. Teapot, Mark 59 (1886), Worcester Border and Center. $80.00-100.00.

PLATE 265. Teapot, 6″h., unmarked, Pictorial Border, Two Temples II Simplified, pattern on body, Polychromed. $75.00-85.00.

PLATE 266. Teapot, Musical type, unmarked. $40.00-50.00.

PLATE 267. Texas Cup, 5½"h., 8½"d., marked "JAPAN". $15.00-20.00.

PLATE 268. Tin, 7½″h., English, Modern. $5.00-7.00.

PLATE 269. Tin (Spice), 3½″h., English, Modern. $2.00-4.00.

PLATE 271. Toaster, 7″h., 7″w., American, by Pan Electrical Mfg. Co., of Cleveland, Ohio. $125.00-150.00.

PLATE 270. Tins (Pill), 2½″l., 2″w., English, Modern. $2.00-4.00.

PLATE 272. Toast Cover or Warmer, 3½"h., 6"d., Mark 106. $35.00-45.00.

PLATE 273. Tobys, 5½"h., left, Mark 63; right, English, unmarked. $175.00-200.00 each.

LEFT: Staffordshire England (unidentified)

143

x4

PLATE 274. Toothpick Holder, 2¼"h.,
American, Buffalo China Script Mark.
$25.00-30.00.
Paid - 5-5-2?

PLATE 275. Trivet, Japanese.
$20.00-25.00.

PLATE 276. Trivet, 5½"d., English,
unmarked. $30.00-35.00.

PLATE 277. Tumbler, Frosted Glass
(set of 6), by General Housewares,
Modern. $1.00-2.00 each; 6 for
$5.00-8.00.

PLATE 278. Tumblers, plastic (set of 8), 4¼"h., by Superlatives, Modern. $7.00-10.00, set of 8.

PLATE 279. Tureen, English, marked "Semi-China" in a square. $350.00-400.00.

PLATE 280. Tureen, 15″h., 11″w., Mark 62. $500.00-550.00.

Unidentified

PLATE 281. Tureen, 9″l., 6″w., English, unmarked. $250.00-300.00.

PLATE 282. Vase, 5″h., unmarked, Japanese. $35.00-45.00.

PLATE 283. Covered Vegetable Dish, 10″l., 8½″w., Mark 7. $65.00-75.00.

Allerton 1929-1942

PLATE 284. Covered Vegetable Dish, 6″h., 12″l., rectangular shape, Mark 7.
$65.00-75.00. *Allerton 1929-1942*

PLATE 285. Open Vegetable, rectangular shape, Mark 4: 7″, $20.00-25.00; 8″,
$25.00-30.00; 9″, $30.00-35.00.

Allerton 1892

PLATE 286. Open Vegetable, round with scalloped edge, Mark 4: 8″, $35.00-40.00; 10″ & 10½″, $45.00-50.00.

Allerton 1890

PLATE 287. Covered Vegetable, 4″h., 9½″d., Mark 9, Booth's pattern. $75.00-85.00.

Booth's 1912

PLATE 288. Open Vegetable, 10″l., Mark 55, Bow Knot Border, Booth's Variant Center Pattern, Polychromed. Pattern name in mark is "Peking". $45.00-55.00.

PLATE 289. Open Vegetable, oval shape, Mark 9 Booth's pattern: 10″l., $40.00-45.00; 8½″l. (not shown), $30.00-35.00.

PLATE 290. Open Vegetable, round shape, Mark 9, Booth's pattern: 9″d., $35.00-40.00; 8″d. (not shown), $30.00-35.00.

PLATE 291. Round Nested Vegetable Bowls, Mark 20: 7″d., $55.00-65.00; 8″d., $65.00-75.00; 9″d., $75.00-85.00.

PLATE 292. Oval Vegetable, 8½″l., Mark 48. $20.00-25.00.

PLATE 293. Wall Plaque, 7″ Brass plate with Willow pattern framed in 2¼″w. oak frame, English. $60.00-70.00.

PLATE 294. Wash Set, Bowl and Pitcher, Mark 20. $500.00-600.00.

PLATE 295. Wash Set: Bowl, 14¼″d.; Pitcher, 10″h., English, marked "Semi-China" in a square and B.T. & S.E.B. and Crown impressed mark, Two Temples II pattern on body, Butterfly Border. $500.00-600.00.

PLATE 296. Wash Set: Bowl, 16″d; Pitcher, 10″h., Mark 53 plus "WEDGWOOD" incised mark. $500.00-600.00.

PLATE 297. Wash Set Chamber Pot, 5½″h., 9¼″d., Mark 20, Flow Blue, goes with Plate 294. $150.00-175.00.

PLATE 298. Wash Set Chamber Pot, goes with Plate 296. $125.00-150.00.

PLATE 299. Wash Set Chamber Pot, Tin, English, unmarked. $60.00-75.00.

PLATE 300. Wash Set Chamber Pot, 5½″h., 11″d., Mark 53 (without Etruria). $125.00-150.00.

PLATE 301. Waste Bowl, 3″h., 6″d., English. $30.00-40.00.

PLATE 302. Waste Bowl, 3½″h., 6½″d., Mark 20, Flow Blue. $45.00-55.00.

PLATE 303. Whiskey Decanter, 8″h., Modern. $20.00-25.00.

GLOSSARY

Bisque - unglazed porcelain.

Body - the clay composition of an article.

Bone China - a ceramic class whose principal ingredient is an ash made from the calcined bones of animals. The bone ash makes up at least 50% of the ingredients for the paste mixture with such materials as china clay and feldspar composing the rest. Josiah Spode I was the inventor of this form of ceramic body in the late 1700's. Bone china is translucent and considered a form of porcelain. England is the primary producer of bone china.

Bow Knot - a border characteristic found on Blue Willow patterns.

China - a term frequently used for any kind of ceramic, but appropriately refers only to true or hard paste porcelain.

Cobalt - an ore found in copper, silver, or tin mines. An oxide formed from this mineral produces a substance used for coloring ceramics known as cobalt blue.

Crazing - a network of fine lines caused by heat or age, appearing on the glaze of earthenwares.

Earthenware - pottery having a porosity of more than 5%. It is made from many different types of natural clays including kaolin, ball clay, and cornish stone. Earthenwares are opaque and may be glazed or unglazed.

Fishroe - a term referring to the outer border characteristic of several Blue Willow border patterns composed of a series of squares or circles with dots in the middle.

Glaze - a liquid substance applied to ceramic bodies for decorative purposes and/or to achieve vitreosity.

Hard Paste - a class of ceramics whose primary ingredient is kaolin, a type of earth containing hydrated aluminum silicates. Kaolin accounts for 50% of the paste with feldspar being the other main ingredient. Hard paste porcelain is fired at extremely high temperatures. It is called "hard" because of the high temperature firing. Hard paste is also referred to as true or natural porcelain since its chief components exist naturally in the earth. Hard paste porcelain is translucent and vitreous if glazed. It is very strong and does not craze.

Impressed - a term referring to marks that are made in the form of a stamp and pressed into the body of a ceramic body before it is fired.

Incised - a term referring to marks that are sharply cut into the clay body of an object before it is fired.

Ironstone - a type of stoneware patented by Mason in England in 1813. Iron slag is pulverized and mixed with the clay to form this type of ceramic body.

Monochrome - one color decoration.

Nankin - the inner border on willow pattern ceramics.

Opaque - meaning that light cannot pass through an object.

Overglaze - refers to decoration, either handpainted or transfer, applied to a ceramic object after a glaze has been applied and fired on an object. Overglaze decoration shows wear through time and can be damaged.

Paste - the clay mixture used to form the body of ceramic objects.

Polychrome - the use of more than one color in decorating ceramic items.

Porcelain - ceramics that are translucent and usually vitreous. The term usually refers to true or hard paste porcelain.

Pottery - any object made of clay and fired at a high termperature.

Printed Marks - marks that are simple handpainted initials or marks, either initial forms or more elaborate, made in the form of a stamp or transfer that can be applied to a ceramic body either over or under the glaze.

Semi-Porcelain - earthenware ceramics. Semi-porcelain objects are opaque and non-vitreous.

Spur Marks - supports made from clay to support and separate ceramic plates and platters in the kiln during the firing process.

Staffordshire Knot - a printed mark in the form of a bow used by many Staffordshire potters during the 19th century (see Mark 63).

Stoneware - pottery which has a porosity of less than 5%. It is fired at extremely high temperatures. The body is glazed and fired only once until the object is vitrified. Stoneware is made from natural stoneware clays which are of a sedimentary type, fine grained, and quite plastic. Stoneware is opaque, heavy, and quite durable.

Transfer - a method of decorating ceramics where a design is engraved on a copper plate. The lines of the design are filled with paint, and the plate is placed on a hot copper plate. A tissue paper is placed over the design. The tissue paper is covered with a soapy mixture which is pressed into the engraved design and taken off and placed (transferred) to an object upside down. The object has been coated with a varnish and is also heated so that the pattern will stick. The pattern is rubbed hard onto the object, and when the piece is dry the paper is washed off.

Translucent - meaning that light can pass through This term refers to the chief characteristic of porcelain.

Underglaze - refers to decoration applied to the body of a ceramic object before a glaze is applied. Patterns or decoration applied under the glaze either by handpainting or transfer method become permanent and cannot be destroyed.

Vitreous - meaning glass-like. This state is achieved on ceramic bodies by glazes made of glass forming materials that are applied to the ceramic body and fired at a high temperature until the body of the object and glaze fuse together becoming one entity.

BIBLIOGRAPHY

Altman, Seymour and Violet. *The Book of Buffalo Pottery*. New York, Bonanza Books, 1969.

Andacht, Sandra, Nancy Garthe, and Robert Mascarelli. *Wallace-Homestead Price Guide to Oriental Antiques*. Des Moines, Iowa, Wallace-Homestead Book Company, 1981.

Barber, Edwin Atlee. *Marks of American Potters*. First published in 1904, reprinted in 1976 by Feingold and Lewis, New York.

Biernacki, Conrad. "As Yet Uncharted Boundaries: The Willow Borders", *The Willow Notebook*, January, 1981.

——————. "The Butterfly Border", *The Willow Notebook*, November, 1981.

——————. "Willow Pattern China", *National Journal*, April, 1982.

Biernacki, Conrad and Connie Rogers. "More on Borders: A Full House Now", *The Willow Notebook*, May, 1981.

——————. "Willow Centre Patterns", *The Willow Notebook*, September, 1981.

——————. "Willow Centre Patterns (addendum)", *The Willow Notebook*, September, 1982.

Boger, Louise Ade. *The Dictionary of World Pottery and Porcelain*. New York, Charles Scribner's Sons, 1971.

Burgess, A.M. *History of the Willow Pattern*. Published privately, 1904.

Copeland, Robert. *Spode's Willow Pattern and other Designs after the Chinese*. New York, Rizzoli, 1980.

Coysh, A.W. *Blue and White Transfer Ware 1780-1840*. Rutland, Vermont, Charles E. Tuttle Company, 1971.

Gaston, Mary Frank. *The Collector's Encyclopedia of Limoges Porcelain*. Paducah, Kentucky, Collector Books, 1980.

Godden, Geoffrey A. *Victorian Porcelain*. New York, Thomas Nelson & Sons, 1961.

——————. *British Pottery and Porcelain, 1780-1850*. New York, A.S. Barnes and Co., Inc., 1963.

——————. *Encyclopedia of British Pottery and Porcelain Marks*. New York, Crown Publishers, 1964.

——————. *The Handbook of British Pottery & Porcelain Marks*. New York, Frederick A. Praeger, 1968.

——————. *Godden's Guide to English Porcelain*. London, Hart-Davis, MacGibbon, Granada Publishing, 1978.

——————. *Oriental Export Market Porcelain*. London, Granada, 1979.

Hughes, G. Bernard. *The Collector's Pocket Book of China*. New York, Award Books; London, Tandem Books, 1965.

Jenkins, Dorothy A. *The Woman's Day Book of Antiques & Collectibles*. Patterson, New Jersey, The Main Street Press William Case House, 1981.

Kovel, Ralph M., and Terry H. *Dictionary of Marks, Pottery and Porcelain*. New York, Crown Publishers, Inc., 1953.

Lehner, Lois. *Ohio Pottery and Glass, Marks and Manufacturers*. Des Moines, Iowa, Wallace-Homestead, 1978.

Little, W.A. *Staffordshire Blue*. London, B.T. Batsford, Ltd., 1969.

Misiewicz, Lois (ed.), *The Willow Notebook*, Number 11-28, January 1980-November 1982.

Poche, Emanuel. *Porcelain Marks of the World*. New York, Arco Publishing Company, Inc., 1974.

Rogers, Connie. "Willow Ware from Ohio", *National Journal*, August, 1981.

—————————. "Blue Willow Plates", *Depression Glass Daze*, September, 1981.

—————————. "More Blue Willow Grill Plates", *Depression Glass Daze*, August, 1982.

Rogers, Connie and Conrad Biernacki. "Willow Borders Illustrated I and II", *The Willow Notebook*, July, 1981.

Sandon, Henry. *Royal Worcester Porcelain from 1862 to the Present Day*. London, Barrie & Jenkins, 1973.

Van Patten, Joan F. *The Collector's Encyclopedia of Nippon Porcelain*. Paducah, Kentucky, Collector Books, 1979.

Worth, Veryl Marie. *Willow Pattern China*. Revised 2nd edition. H.S. Worth Co., 1979. Distributed by Fact Book Company, Oakridge, Oregon.

—————————. *Collectors Price Guide to Willow Pattern China*, 1981. Distributed by Fact Book Company, Oakridge, Oregon.